D0116511

EDGE BOOKS

LIONS

BIG CATS

BY TAMMY GAGNE

Consultant: Christina Simmons
San Diego Zoo Global
San Diego, California

CAPSTONE PRESS
a capstone imprint

Edge Books are published by Capstone Press,
1710 Roe Crest Drive, North Mankato, Minnesota 56003.
www.capstonepub.com

Books published by Capstone Press are manufactured with paper
containing at least 10 percent post-consumer waste.

Library of Congress Cataloging-in-Publication Data
Gagne, Tammy.
 Lions / by Tammy Gagne.
  p. cm. – (Edge books. Big cats)
 Includes bibliographical references and index.
 ISBN 978-1-4296-7643-4 (library binding)
 1. Lion—Juvenile literature. I. Title.
 QL737.C23G347 2012
 599.757—dc22   2011010830

Editorial Credits
Brenda Haugen, editor; Kyle Grenz, designer; Svetlana Zhurkin,
    media researcher; Laura Manthe, production specialist

Photo Credits 4976 1207 11/12
Alamy: AfriPics, 11; Digital Stock, 5; Digital Vision, 13; Dreamstime: Callan
Chesser, 18, Federicoriz, 19, 22–23, Rene Olsthoorn, 14–15; National Geographic
Stock: Frans Lanting, 10; Newscom: Danita Delimont Photography/Ralph H.
Bendjebar, 25; Shutterstock: Aperture Untamed, 24, EcoPrint, cover, Eric Isselée,
16, 20, 21, Jason Prince, 4, 28–29, JKlingebiel, 17, Johan1966, 12, Keith Levit, 9
(bottom), Matej Hudovernik, 6–7, Melissa Schalke, 1, Michal Baranski, 9 (top),
Natursports, 27, Stanislav Eduardovich Petrov (background), throughout

Printed in the United States of America in Stevens Point, Wisconsin.
102011   006404WZS12

TABLE OF CONTENTS

Chapter 1

MIGHT AND MANE

The sun is setting on another scorching day in Africa. Antelope stop for one last drink at the nearest watering hole. A few stray from the herd, but the smart ones stick together. Perhaps they know the lions are just waking up.

It's easy to see why the lion is often called the king of the beasts. Lions are among the largest cats in the world. Male lions weigh between 350 and 500 pounds (159 to 227 kilograms). Their bodies are between 5 and 8 feet (1.5 and 2.4 meters) long. Females, or lionesses, are smaller. They weigh from 250 to 400 pounds (113 and 181 kg) and measure about 5 feet (1.5 m) long. A lion's tail is usually between 24 and 36 inches (61 and 91 centimeters) long.

Size Comparison Chart

The average height of an American male is 5 feet, 10 inches (178 cm).

THE MANE EVENT

It isn't just a lion's size that makes it look like royalty. Like everything else about a lion, its head is huge. Adult male lions have manes. This long, thick fur surrounds the animal's head and makes the lion look even larger than he is. A male lion's mane isn't just for looks. It also protects the lion's neck from the claws of other animals during fights.

Big Cat Fact

Male lions without manes have been discovered in some parts of eastern Africa. Scientists believe these lions may have adapted to their climate. Without manes, the lions stay cooler in the higher temperatures of this area.

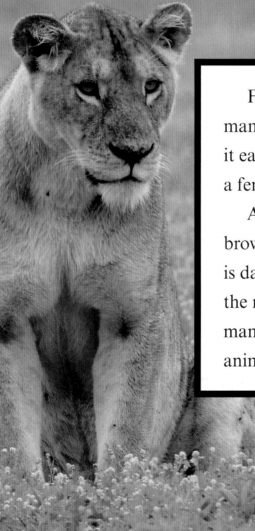

Female lions do not have manes. This difference makes it easy to tell a male lion from a female.

All lions have short sandy brown fur. A male's mane is darker than the fur on the rest of its body. A lion's mane often gets darker as the animal grows older.

LION LIFE

Lions live in Africa from Senegal to Somalia. They are also found in the southern areas of the continent. Many lions live in the savanna, a flat grassy area with few trees. But some have **habitats** in the mountains of Ethiopia and Kenya.

Big Cat Fact

The natural life span of a lion in the wild is about 15 years. Wild females usually live a few years longer than males. Lions in zoos can live up to 30 years.

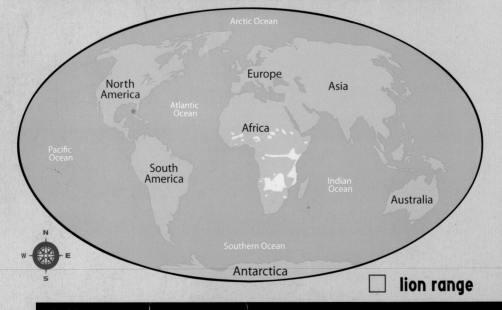

☐ **lion range**

habitat—the natural place and natural conditions in which an animal or plant lives

Asian Lions

The only wild lions outside of Africa live in Asia. Asian lions were saved from dying out by the Nawab of Junagadh, an Indian governor, in 1913. Today about 300 of these lions live in India's Sasan-Gir National Park. Their home is a 445-square-mile (1,153-square-kilometer) sanctuary.

sanctuary—a place where animals are cared for and protected

Chapter 2

WHEN THE SUN GOES DOWN

Lions are the only large cats that live in groups. A group of lions is called a pride. A pride can include as many as 40 lions. The females outnumber the males. A pride may include up to seven adult males and 20 adult females and their cubs. But most prides consist of about 12 lions. In rare situations, an adult lion will live alone. For example, a lioness may leave the pride to give birth.

Big Cat Fact

A lion pride's territory can be as large as 100 square miles (259 sq. km).

A pride's male lions usually aren't related. The males protect the pride. The more males a pride has, the greater the pride's chance for survival.

The female members of a pride are often related. The group usually includes mothers, daughters, and sisters. The females raise young and hunt.

Female lions hunt in groups. By working together, they are better able to catch fast **prey**, such as antelope, wildebeests, and zebras. This teamwork ends when the females bring dinner home to the pride. It is common for lions to argue over which animal eats first. The older males almost always win these fights. The cubs eat after the other lions are done.

prey—an animal hunted by another animal for food

ON THE PROWL

Lions are fearless hunters. They will attack any animal they think they can kill. How big or mean the animal is doesn't seem to matter. Lions may hunt buffalo, crocodiles, giraffes, hippos, rhinos, and wild hogs. If food is scarce, lions will even attack an elephant.

Leadership Skills

Female lions often have different strengths. Some female members of a pride are better at hunting certain animals. Some may be better at hunting in certain terrain, such as open areas. The best lioness for the job takes the lead on a hunt.

Lions are **nocturnal**. They rest most of the day. They do most of their hunting at night. When females leave the pride at dusk, they may not return until dawn. The hot sun makes hunting more difficult during the day. The cooler night air is more comfortable for lions. Darkness also allows lions to sneak up on their prey without being seen.

Big Cat Fact

When a lion chases its prey, it can reach speeds of up to 50 miles (80 km) per hour.

IT PAYS TO BE KING

Sometimes lions let other animals do the hunting for them. Lions often steal the kills of smaller predators. Lions are known to be **scavengers**. When food is scarce, more than half a lion's diet may be found or stolen food.

scavenger—an animal that feeds on animals that are already dead

Big Cat Fact

Lions lie down when they eat. After eating a large meal, a lion may sleep for up to 24 hours.

Both in the mountains and in the savanna, the adult lion sits at the top of the food chain. It has no predators. A wandering cub can become the prey of a hyena or leopard, but no other animals hunt adult lions.

Chapter 3

SIGHTS AND SOUNDS

Lions have great eyesight. They can see five times better than people can. Lions use their keen eyesight to spy prey from great distances. Their round eyes are also perfect for hunting at night. The shape allows more light to enter the lion's eyes, which improves night vision.

Lions also are very sensitive to smells. They use more than their noses for detecting scents. Like all cats, a lion has a **Jacobson's organ** at the top of its mouth. When taking in a scent, a lion will open its mouth. Doing so allows the Jacobson's organ to work. A lion uses its sense of smell for hunting and for locating the kills of other predators.

A lion also uses scents to mark territory. A lion will urinate on trees in the area where its pride lives and hunts. It may also stay away from territory that lions from other prides have marked.

Big Cat Fact

Other animals with Jacobson's organs include bison, dogs, elephants, goats, lizards, snakes, mice, rats, and pigs.

Jacobson's organ—an odor-detecting organ inside the mouths of some animals

17

I CAN HEAR YOU!

Lions have very good hearing. They can sense sounds from more than 1 mile (1.6 km) away. Like other cats, a lion can also tell the direction from which a sound comes. It moves its ears around to detect the source of a noise. When a lion roars, it can be heard from up to 5 miles (8 km) away. Another lion can tell where the roaring lion is located.

Lions roar to claim territory. Lions are one of only four cats that roar. The others are the jaguar, leopard, and tiger. When many animals hear a lion's roar, they move in another direction. When lions from one pride hear another pride's roars, they may roar back in answer.

Living with Lions

How do we know so much about lions? Many people have made it their life's work to learn as much as possible about these wild cats. Some have even lived alongside them. In 1974 Mark and Delia Owens traveled to the Central Kalahari Game Reserve in Botswana to study lions. They spent seven years living in tents in the African wilderness. They wrote about their experiences in a book called *Cry of the Kalahari*. Their work was dangerous. But without people like them, we likely wouldn't know as much about lions as we do today.

Big Cat Fact

Lions are often copycats! When one lion yawns, the other lions in the pride will often yawn too. They also tend to groom themselves and roar after one lion starts the behavior.

Chapter 4

RAISING CUBS

Shortly before giving birth, a female lion usually leaves her pride and finds a safe den. A female lion usually gives birth to between one and six cubs. Though rare, litters as large as nine have been reported. In most of these cases, only four or five cubs survive.

Big Cat Fact

Cubs born into a pride are twice as likely to survive as cubs of a lioness living on her own.

Each cub weighs about 3.5 pounds (1.6 kg). Cubs are born with full coats of fur. Sometimes they have spots. These markings usually fade as the cubs get older. Cubs' eyes open between 3 and 11 days of age. They begin eating meat around 3 months of age.

Mother lions are very protective of their cubs. They don't let other lions near the cubs for the first few weeks. Once the mother has rejoined the pride, the female lions share the job of raising the young.

GROWING UP

When the cubs are between 9 months and 1 year old, they start tagging along on hunts. When the cubs play, they copy many of the behaviors they see during hunts. This is one way the cubs practice what they have learned.

By the time a male lion is 2 years old, its mane will start growing. When the adult males notice this change, they may drive the young males out of the pride. But many males stay with their first pride for more than three years. Then it's time for these adult males to find prides of their own. Female cubs tend to stay with their prides their entire lives.

Big Cat Fact

About 80 percent of lion cubs die before their second birthday. The biggest threats they face are starvation and male lions. When male lions take over a new pride, they will often kill the pride's cubs.

Chapter 5

WILD POPULATIONS

The world's lion population has been decreasing for many years. In the 1990s about 100,000 lions lived in Africa. Today fewer than 30,000 lions remain. Many factors have caused this sharp drop in numbers.

Severe droughts have caused the deaths of many lions. Some animals have died from lack of water. Others have died from diseases. Without water, lions have a hard time battling illnesses.

One big threat to the health of lions is **bovine tuberculosis**. This deadly disease kills prey animals, such as buffalo. Prey can also pass the illness to lions. If too many animals become infected, the disease could lower the lion population.

Another factor that affects lion populations is loss of habitat. An increase in human population has caused a greater need for farming. New farms and ranches have taken land away from the lions. When the lions return to the land they once called home, they are often killed by the ranchers. **Poachers** have also played a part in the population decline.

bovine tuberculosis—a disease that affects the lungs of cattle

poacher—a person who hunts or fishes illegally

SAVING LIONS

Conservation groups are working with ranchers to help maintain lion populations. At night, ranchers can use thorny enclosures called bomas to keep livestock in and lions out.

Conservation groups are also trying to get ranchers more involved in tourism. Tour groups travel through Africa to see lions and other animals. If ranchers receive some of the money these tourists spend, ranchers may help keep lion populations from dropping.

Big Cat Fact

The Lions Guardians is a program of the Living with Lions conservation group. Volunteers called guardians teach animal herders ways to avoid lions. They also show ranchers how to improve livestock pens. Most important, the program teaches people in Africa about the importance of not killing lions.

conservation—the protection of animals and plants, as well as the wise use of natural resources

Drought and disease will continue to strike, but the unnecessary killing of lions can be stopped. The people of Africa must share their land with lions if these cats are going to survive. Sometimes even kings need a little help.

Saving African Animals

The Born Free Foundation works to protect various types of animals from dying out. The group uses the money it collects to start wildlife preserves. This land gives lions and other animals protected habitats in Botswana, Kenya, Tanzania, Zambia, and Zimbabwe. People cannot build or hunt in these special areas.

The Born Free Foundation also helps to solve conflicts between people and lions. Members of the group teach farmers how to protect their livestock from lions without killing the big cats.

Big Cat Fact

The Born Free Foundation is named after the book *Born Free* by Joy Adamson. The book tells the true story of an orphaned lion cub. Adamson and her husband, George, named the cub Elsa and raised her to adulthood. They then helped her go back to the wild.

GLOSSARY

bovine tuberculosis (BOH-vine too-bur-kyuh-LOH-sis)—a disease that affects the lungs of cattle

conservation (kahn-sur-VAY-shun)—the protection of animals and plants, as well as the wise use of natural resources

drought (DROUT)—a long period of weather with little or no rainfall

habitat (HAB-uh-tat)—the natural place and natural conditions in which an animal or plant lives

Jacobson's organ (JAY-cub-sunz OR-gun)—an odor-detecting organ inside the mouths of some animals

nocturnal (nok-TUR-nuhl)—active at night and resting during the day

poacher (POHCH-ur)—a person who hunts or fishes illegally

predator (PRED-uh-tur)—an animal that hunts other animals for food

prey (PRAY)—an animal hunted by another animal for food

sanctuary (SANGK-choo-er-ee)—a place animals are cared for and protected

scavenger (SKAV-uhn-jer)—an animal that feeds on animals that are already dead

READ MORE

Joubert, Beverly, and Dereck Joubert. *Face to Face with Lions.* Washington, D.C.: National Geographic, 2008.

Knowles, Ruth. *Christian the Lion: Based on the Amazing and Heartwarming True Story.* New York: Delacorte Press, 2009.

Riley, Joelle. *African Lions.* Animals. Minneapolis: Lerner Publications, 2008.

INTERNET SITES

FactHound offers a safe, fun way to find Internet sites related to this book. All of the sites on FactHound have been researched by our staff.

Here's all you do:

Visit *www.facthound.com*

Type in this code: 9781429676434

 Check out projects, games and lots more at **www.capstonekids.com**

31

INDEX